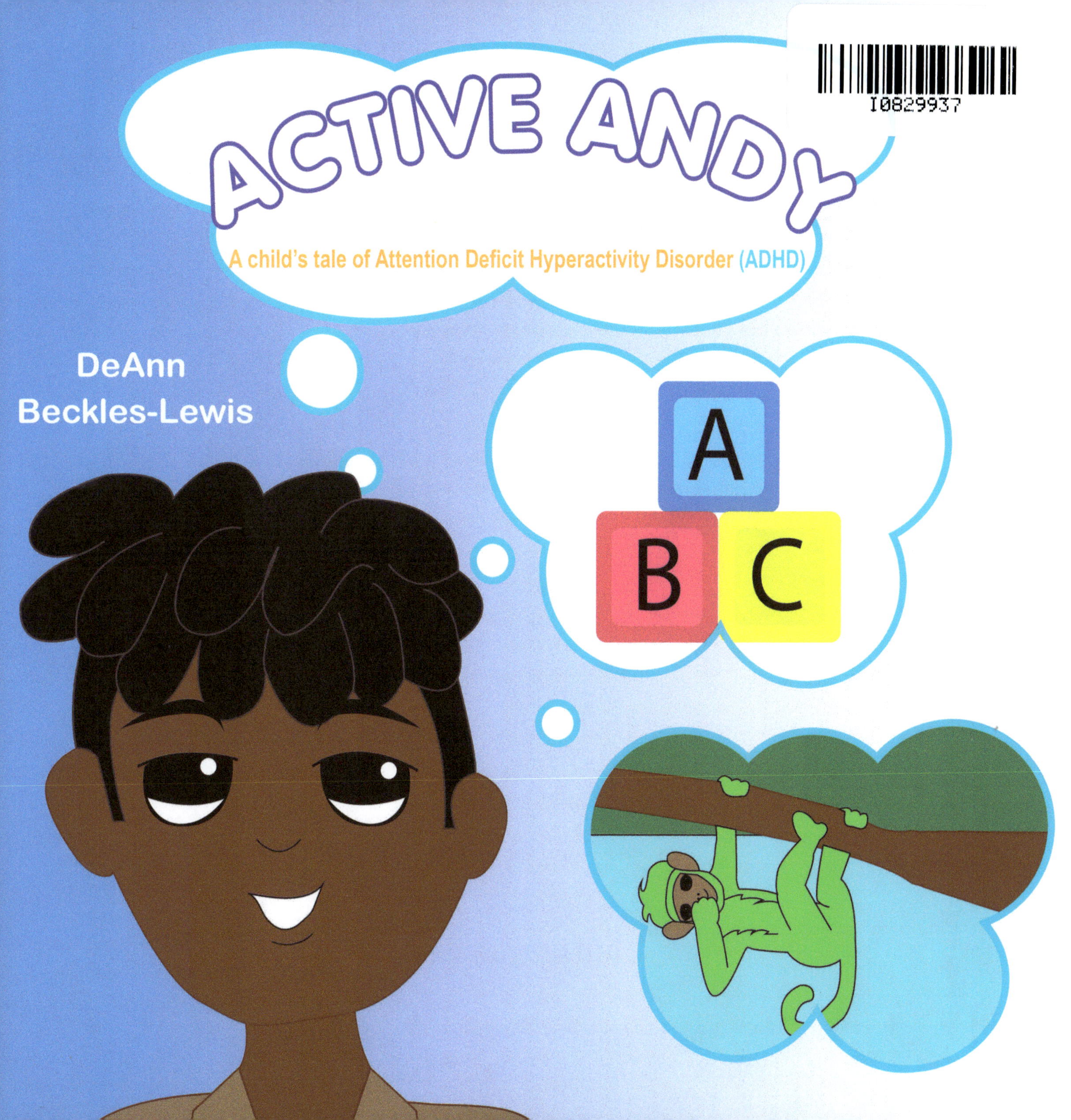

ACTIVE ANDY
A child's tale of Attention Deficit Hyperactivity Disorder (ADHD)
DeAnn Beckles-Lewis
A
B C
I0829937

AuthorHouse™
1663 Liberty Drive
Bloomington, IN 47403
www.authorhouse.com
Phone: 1 (800) 839-8640

Illustrations by Geaver Cox

This book is printed on acid-free paper.

ISBN: 978-1-7283-4736-3 (sc)
ISBN: 978-1-7283-4737-0 (e)

Print information available on the last page.

Published by AuthorHouse 02/14/2020

authorHOUSE®

Active Andy

A child's tale of Attention Deficit
Hyperactivity Disorder (ADHD)

Hello my name is Andy. I am 8 years old. I look like all the other boys, but sometimes it is not easy being me.

I don't do well at school. I think I am smart but sometimes there seems to be so much things going on. Oh, is that a monkey in that tree? See what I mean?

I am ALWAYS in trouble with my teacher. He tells me to stay still and pay attention but no matter how hard I try, I can't just stay still and follow the lesson.

At home, it is pretty much the same thing. I am always on the go. After all, there is so much to see and even more to do. My mother says that I have a motor and that I'm naughty. I don't mean to be. I do have a lot of energy and I love to play. I do sit still during my favorite cartoons. I love to sit in front of the television with my toys and pretend that I am in the cartoon, doing all the cool tricks.

Afterwards I normally get a snack. Hmmm candy is my favorite. Dad asked me if I have ants in my pants, but I don't see any. I get punished A LOT!!

When my mother took me to the doctor for my check-up, she told Dr. Grant that I was driving her crazy and that she didn't know how to handle me. I felt so sad. Dr. Grant then sent me over to another doctor in her building. She called her the Psychologist. I was scared; for sure I was in big trouble now.

The psychologist was Dr. Miller. She was smiling when I came into the room. She took me over to her toys and said that I could play while she spoke to my mom. When she was finished, she came back for me. I guessed I must have looked scared, because she told me not to be scared and that I was not in any trouble. Dr. Miller said that she was there to help me *be the best me.* We played, and talked and did some activities. Some of the activities were easy and some were hard, but it was fun. Dr. Miller said once I did my best she was happy. She gave my mom something to do, so I was not the only one with stuff to do. When we were finished, Dr. Miller sat me down with my mother to explain what was wrong and what can *be* done to make things better.

My problems were mainly due to a condition the psychologist called Attention Deficit Hyperactivity Disorder or ADHD. ADHD is a condition some people have where they find it hard to focus on one thing at a time. It may be hard to stay still while sitting or standing and you may act quickly without thinking. Children with ADHD may find it hard to complete tasks and have to work harder to keep up their grades than others. That definitely sounded like me.

I still go to see Dr. Miller. She is teaching me
how to handle my problem. I use different games
and tricks to help me to focus and stay in one
place long enough to do what I need to.

I also had to cut back on my snacks – bye-bye candy. Not everything we have tried worked, but I think we found the right stuff and I am doing much better. I even got a star at school. Even mother says she knows how to handle me now. I still get punished but not as much.

Report
Art   A+
Math   B+
English B
Science A-

Some children have to take medication so they can slow down, and not have so much trouble with following rules and doing school work. I was happy when both Dr. Miller and Dr. Grant agreed that I don't have to take medicine.

"I am Andy, and because of the help from everyone for my ADHD, it is easier to be me now."

Parents' Note:

Attention Deficit Hyperactivity Disorder is a psychological disorder associated with inattention, hyperactivity and impulsivity. It can be stressful dealing with a child with untreated ADHD. If you suspect that your child is experiencing symptoms similar to those of the disorder, please consult your pediatrician. Please note that there are several disorders which are similar to ADHD, therefore it is best that your child is diagnosed by trained professional. Early diagnosis means early treatment and a better outcome for the child.